FROM SAWDUST TO SALES
HOW TO MARKET AND MANAGE YOUR CABINETRY BUSINESS

BUILT TO LAST: LESSONS IN OPERATING A
CUSTOM CABINET SHOP
BOOK TWO

JASON DORR

Copyright © 2023 by jason dorr

All rights reserved.

No part of this book may be reproduced in any form or by any electronic or mechanical means, including information storage and retrieval systems, without written permission from the author, except for the use of brief quotations in a book review.

FOREWORD

I once watched a cabinetmaker spend fourteen hours on a single door panel — scribing, fitting, sanding to a standard most people would never notice. The craftsmanship was extraordinary. His business, though, was quietly failing. He had no idea what his jobs were actually costing him. He relied entirely on word-of-mouth and crossed his fingers that the phone would ring. When it didn't, he dropped his prices. He was, without knowing it, working harder every year to earn less.

That cabinetmaker is not unusual. I've met versions of him all over the industry — skilled, proud, dedicated, and completely unprepared for the business side of the work. The trade schools teach joinery and finishing. Nobody teaches you how to price a kitchen, how to find the customers who will actually pay what your work is worth, or how to build a business that isn't dependent on your showing up every day just to keep it alive.

That's what this book is for.

It's not a generic marketing textbook with the word "cabinetry" dropped in every few pages. It's written from inside the trade — for shops of five people, for the one-man operation that wants to grow, for the craftsman who is good at the work but knows they need to get better at the business of the work. The strategies here are specific to how cabinet shops actually run: the long sales cycles, the contractor relationships, the challenge of photographing dark walnut for Instagram, the cash flow gap between when you buy materials and when the customer pays.

Read the chapters that apply to where you are right now. Return to the others when you're ready. The surveys and templates in the appendix are meant to be used, not just read.

The goal isn't to turn you into a marketer. The goal is to build a business strong enough that you get to keep doing the work you love.

Best regards,
    Jason

CHAPTER 1
THE CABINET SHOP PARADOX

The skills that make someone a great cabinetmaker and the skills that make someone a successful cabinet shop owner are almost directly opposed.

A great cabinetmaker slows down to get it right. A good business owner knows when "right" is costing more than the job is worth. A great cabinetmaker is perfectionistic, detail-obsessed, and happy to work alone. A good business owner delegates, simplifies, and spends time talking to people. A great cabinetmaker values the work itself above almost everything. A good business owner sometimes has to make decisions that protect the business even when they feel wrong for the work.

This isn't a criticism of cabinetmakers. It's an acknowledgment that most of us got into this trade because of the work, not the business — and that the business demands a different part of you than the shop does.

The most common trap is what I'd call the word-of-mouth ceiling. Most custom cabinet shops are built almost entirely on referrals. The shop does good work, the customers tell their friends, the phone rings. It feels sustainable right up until it isn't. A slow winter, a key referral source who moves away or retires, a general contractor who finds someone cheaper — and suddenly the pipeline is empty. At that point, most shops panic and discount. They take on jobs below their actual cost because they don't know what their actual cost is. They survive the slow period but emerge from it with less money and less confidence.

Good word-of-mouth gets you started. A real marketing strategy is what keeps you from ending up at the mercy of whoever happened to call this week.

The other common failure is underpricing. Custom cabinetry is a premium product. The materials are expensive, the labor is skilled, and the production time is long. Yet many shops price by gut feel, by what competitors charge, or by what they think a customer will pay — rather than by what it actually costs to produce the work and run the business. A shop doing $400,000 a year in revenue but netting less than $30,000 after expenses isn't a successful business. It's an expensive hobby.

This book addresses both problems directly. The marketing chapters will help you build a system that generates leads without relying entirely on who happened to call last. The financial and operations chapters will help you understand what your work actually costs so you can price it to build a business, not just fill a schedule.

The Underpricing Trap — and Why It's So Hard to Escape

Most cabinetmakers underprice their work. Not by a little — often by 20 to 40 percent. And most of them know it, in a vague, uncomfortable way, without fully admitting it to themselves because admitting it would force a reckoning they're not sure they're ready for.

The underpricing trap has several entry points. The first is competitive anxiety: you look at what the shop down the road charges, assume they must know something you don't, and price near them. The second is customer pressure: a homeowner winces at a quote and you shave a few hundred dollars off to close the job, which feels like a reasonable accommodation in the moment and becomes a habit that reshapes your entire pricing over years. The third is the most insidious — a deep cultural belief, common in the trades, that charging appropriately for skilled work is somehow greedy. That asking for what your work is worth is the same as taking advantage of someone.

It is not. A cabinet shop that underprices its work doesn't stay in business long enough to serve anyone. Pricing correctly isn't a moral failure — it's the prerequisite for being able to keep doing the work at all.

Consider what a full custom kitchen actually involves: design consultations, detailed drawings, material procurement and storage, weeks of shop time on precision machinery operated by skilled tradespeople, finishing work that requires both chemistry knowledge and a practiced eye, transportation, installation in a live home with real people disrupted, and warranty coverage afterward. A shop charging $18,000 for that kitchen is not providing a bargain. They're subsidizing the customer's renovation with their own financial stability, their employees' wages, and ultimately their ability to stay in business.

Price your work to build a business. Anything less is a loan to your customer that you'll never get back.

The escape from the underpricing trap is not raising every price overnight — that creates its own problems. It's building the financial visibility to know what your work actually costs, and then adjusting your pricing incrementally, project type by project type, until your margins match your benchmarks. We'll cover the mechanics of that in Chapter 8.

A Tale of Two Shops

To make this concrete, consider two fictional cabinet shops in the same mid-sized city. Both have been in business about eight years. Both build excellent work. Both have loyal customers who speak highly of them.

Shop A — we'll call it Millbrook Cabinetry — has never formally thought about marketing. Their website was built in 2017 and hasn't been updated. They have six Google reviews. They get almost all their work from referrals, which is great when it's flowing and terrifying when it isn't. In a slow quarter two years ago, they discounted a full kitchen project by $4,200 to close it. They've done similar things three times since. Their revenue last year was $420,000. Their net profit was $21,000 — about 5%. The owner, Mark, works 55 hours a week and took one vacation in the past three years.

Shop B — Harborview Custom — made a different set of decisions. Four years ago, the owner hired a local photographer for $800 to shoot six completed projects. She created a Houzz profile with those photos and asked her ten best customers for reviews. She started posting process photos on Instagram twice a week. She had a conversation with a kitchen designer at an NKBA event and ended up with a design partnership that now sends her four to six jobs per year. She raised her prices by 12% eighteen months ago. Three customers asked about it; none walked away. Her revenue last year was $390,000. Her net profit was $58,000 — nearly 15%. She works 45 hours a week and took two weeks off in the summer.

Millbrook does more revenue. Harborview makes more money. The difference isn't talent — Mark and the

Harborview owner are equally skilled craftspeople. The difference is a set of deliberate decisions about marketing, pricing, and customer selection made over a few years. That's what this book is about.

Why Marketing Feels Uncomfortable for Craftspeople

Ask most cabinetmakers what they think about marketing and they'll use words like "salesy," "fake," or "not what I do." There's a deep cultural tradition in the trades of letting the work speak for itself — which is admirable, and also a liability.

The truth is that marketing for a custom cabinet shop isn't about persuading people to buy something they don't need. It's about making it easier for the right people to find you. It's about showing your work to the homeowners who are already planning a kitchen renovation and just don't know you exist yet. It's about staying in contact with the contractor who used you two years ago so that when a new project comes up, your name is the first one they think of.

When you think of it that way — as communication rather than persuasion — marketing starts to feel a lot more like something a craftsperson can do without feeling like they're selling out. Harborview's owner didn't feel like she was selling when she posted a video of a dovetail being cut in her shop. She was sharing work she was proud of. The marketing was a byproduct of that.

What This Book Covers — and What It Doesn't

This book is organized to follow the lifecycle of a customer: finding them, convincing them, closing the sale, serving them well, and turning them into a source of future business. It also covers the operational and financial foundations that make everything else possible.

What it doesn't cover is the craft itself. It assumes you already know how to build excellent cabinets. It also doesn't cover every detail of business law, accounting, or HR policy — those topics fill their own books. What you'll find here is the specific, practical guidance that applies to the reality of running a custom cabinet shop, with the level of detail that general business books never provide because they aren't written for this trade.

CHAPTER 2
KNOWING YOUR CUSTOMER

There is no such thing as "a cabinetry customer." The homeowner renovating their kitchen and the general contractor building fifty tract houses are both buying cabinets, but they have almost nothing else in common. They find you differently, decide differently, care about different things, and require entirely different approaches to win their business and serve them well.

Most cabinet shops treat all their customers the same way because they've never sat down and thought carefully about who they're actually selling to. This chapter is that exercise.

The Three Customer Types
The Homeowner Renovator

This is the customer most custom cabinet shops think of first. They're planning a kitchen remodel, a bathroom upgrade, a built-in for the living room. They're spending real money — typically $15,000 to $60,000 or more for a full kitchen — and they're doing it once, maybe twice in their lives. That means the stakes feel very high to them.

The homeowner renovator usually starts researching 6 to 12 months before they're ready to buy. They look at Instagram, Pinterest, Houzz, and Google. They ask friends who've recently renovated. They may visit a showroom or two. By the time they call you, they've often already formed strong opinions about what they want — and strong anxieties about getting ripped off, blown past their budget, or stuck with a contractor who disappears mid-project.

Their core fears are: paying too much, not being able to visualize the finished product, and trusting the wrong person. Address all three directly in how you market, how you quote, and how you communicate during the project.

The Kitchen and Bath Designer

Designers are a different category entirely. A kitchen and bath designer with a steady stream of projects can send you more volume than any single homeowner ever could. They're not your customer — they're your distribution channel. Their customer is the homeowner; you're the supplier they trust to make them look good.

Winning a designer relationship requires a different approach than winning a homeowner. Designers care about reliability and finish quality above price. They care about whether you communicate proactively or make them chase you. They care about whether you make them look good or whether you create problems they have to explain to their client. One bad experience and they move on. One excellent experience — especially on a difficult job — and they become loyal for years.

The path to designer relationships is usually personal: attend NKBA (National Kitchen and Bath Association) events, visit local design studios with a portfolio, offer to take a designer to lunch and walk them through your shop. It takes time, but a single strong designer relationship can transform a shop's revenue.

The General Contractor

General contractors are volume buyers. They may not want the most custom, most detailed work — they want reliable, on-time, correctly-built cabinets at a price that fits their project budget. The GC relationship is about trust and consistency more than it is about craftsmanship.

The main challenge with GC work is margin. GCs negotiate hard, expect discounts for volume, and may push you into a commodity pricing dynamic if you let them. The key is to know your costs before entering any contractor conversation, and to be clear about what's included and what isn't. A low-margin GC relationship that fills your shop during slow months can be valuable. A low-margin GC relationship that crowds out higher-margin homeowner work is a trap.

Understanding What Motivates Each Type

Once you know which type of customer you're talking to, you can understand what drives their decisions.

Homeowners are motivated by vision and trust. They want to see what their space could look like, and they want to believe you're the right person to make it happen. Show them beautiful finished work. Give them a clear process. Be responsive and communicative from the first inquiry. The homeowner who feels heard and informed becomes the homeowner who refers you.

Designers are motivated by reputation and reliability. They stake their professional credibility on every vendor they recommend. Show them your quality in person. Deliver on every commitment. When something goes wrong — and it will — communicate immediately and take ownership. Designers forgive problems; they don't forgive surprises.

Contractors are motivated by price, schedule, and not having to think about it. Be competitive on price, be precise on schedule, and make the ordering and communication process as frictionless as possible. If they have to call you to figure out where a job stands, you're already in trouble.

Conducting Market Research

Market research doesn't have to mean formal studies or hired consultants. For a cabinet shop, the most valuable market intelligence usually comes from three places: your existing customers, your local competitors, and the platforms where potential customers look for inspiration.

Learning from Existing Customers

Your current customers know things about your business that you don't. They know what they were nervous about before they called you, what they noticed that impressed them, what they wished had gone differently, and why they picked you over someone else. That last one is particularly valuable — the reason a customer chose you is often not the reason you think they chose you.

The surveys in Appendix A1 (pre-project) and A2 (post-project) are designed to extract exactly this information. Use them. Even getting responses from ten customers will tell you things about how your business is perceived that years of your own guessing won't.

Understanding Your Competitors

Look at the websites and social media of the three to five cabinet shops in your market that most directly compete with you. Notice what they emphasize: do they lead with price, with quality, with speed, with a particular style? Notice what they don't show — that gap may be your opportunity. If none of them show their shop or their process, that's a differentiator available to you.

Also pay attention to their Google and Houzz reviews. Customer complaints on competitor profiles are a direct window into what the market is not getting from existing options. If review after review on your competitor's profile mentions communication problems, and you're genuinely responsive, that's worth more than any marketing copy.

Watching Where Buyers Look

For custom cabinetry, Houzz is more important than most shop owners realize. It's the platform where homeowners specifically planning home improvement projects spend time — meaning the intent level is high. A well-maintained Houzz profile with professional photos and positive reviews can generate steady inbound inquiries at zero ongoing cost. If you're not on Houzz, creating a profile should be one of your first priorities.

Pinterest and Instagram are also important, but they function differently — more as inspiration and awareness platforms than as direct lead generators. We'll cover them in detail in Chapter 4.

Gathering and Using Customer Feedback

The most important thing about customer feedback is not collecting it — it's using it. Many shops send a satisfaction survey after a project, look at the results once, and then file them away. That's not a feedback system. That's paperwork.

A real feedback system feeds directly into how you price, how you communicate, how you handle issues, and what you show potential customers. When a customer tells you the installation was great but the wait for materials felt too long with no communication, that's a process problem. Fix it. When customers consistently mention that they loved seeing the shop before the project started, that's a selling tool. Build it into your discovery process.

See Appendix A1 for a pre-project survey to understand

customer needs, Appendix A2 for a post-project satisfaction survey, and Appendix A3 for a phone script to gather more detailed feedback from customers who want to talk.

CHAPTER 3
STANDING OUT: YOUR BRAND AND MARKETING STRATEGY

Every cabinet shop in your market does roughly what you do. They build cabinets. They have a website. Most of them have some version of "quality craftsmanship" and "custom solutions" in their marketing materials. The question is why someone should call you instead of them — and whether you can answer that question clearly and quickly.

Defining Your Unique Selling Proposition

Your Unique Selling Proposition (USP) is not a tagline. It's not "quality you can trust" or "built to last." Those phrases mean nothing because every competitor says them too. Your USP is the specific, honest answer to: what do you offer that your direct competitors don't?

To find it, stop looking at your marketing and start looking at your business. What do your best customers consistently mention in their reviews? What problems do you solve better than anyone in your market? What do you do differently in your process, your materials, your communication, or your design capabilities?

Here's a worked example. Imagine two shops

competing in the same mid-sized city. Shop A builds excellent cabinets and has been in business fifteen years. Shop B opened four years ago. Shop B noticed that most competitors in their market were strong on production but weak on the design process — customers were often left trying to visualize a finished kitchen from a two-dimensional drawing. Shop B invested in a 3D rendering tool and trained their designer to produce photorealistic room visualizations before a contract was signed. Their close rate on consultations jumped dramatically. That capability became their USP: "You'll see your kitchen in full 3D before you spend a dollar."

Notice what this USP does: it addresses a specific customer fear (not being able to visualize the result), it's verifiable (you can demonstrate it in the first meeting), and it's not easy for a competitor to copy overnight. That's a real differentiator.

Other genuine USPs for cabinet shops include: a two-week lead time when competitors quote six weeks, a finish room that can match any paint color in the Sherwin-Williams or Benjamin Moore system, specialty work in a specific material (white oak, painted shaker, glass-front), or a showroom experience that lets customers touch and compare every hardware option. What's yours?

Once you've identified it, your USP should appear on your website homepage, in every sales conversation, and in any marketing material you produce. It's not a boast — it's an explanation of what makes choosing you the right decision.

One more example worth examining: a small shop in a competitive suburban market noticed that every competitor advertised lead times of ten to fourteen weeks. They streamlined their production process and their material ordering so they could reliably deliver in six weeks for standard projects. They put "Ready in 6 Weeks — Guaranteed" on their website header. Their consultation requests doubled within three months. They hadn't changed what they built. They'd changed how they described an operational advantage they already had but had never thought to communicate.

Creating a Brand that Fits Your Shop

Brand is not a logo. Brand is the total impression your business makes — on a website, in an email, in your shop when a customer visits, in the way your installer introduces himself when he shows up at someone's home. Every one of those touchpoints either reinforces or undermines the image you're trying to project.

The first step is deciding what that image is. Custom cabinet shops generally occupy one of three brand positions: premium craftsmen (high price, high quality, exclusivity), reliable specialists (mid-market, dependable, professional), or value leaders (competitive pricing, standard options, fast turnaround). None of these is wrong — but you cannot occupy all three. Pick the one that matches your actual capabilities and your target customer, and then build everything around it consistently.

A premium craftsman brand uses rich photography, restrained design, and language that emphasizes material quality, detail, and time. A reliable specialist brand emphasizes process, communication, and track record. A value leader brand emphasizes ease, speed, and straightforward pricing. The visual language — your colors, your website design, your photography style — should reflect your position.

Consistency matters more than perfection. A modest but consistent brand builds recognition and trust over time. An inconsistent brand — beautiful photos but slow email responses, premium pricing but a website that looks ten years old — creates cognitive dissonance that kills trust before a relationship can start.

Choosing Your Marketing Channels

Not every marketing channel is right for every shop. The right channels depend on which customer type you're primarily targeting, what your budget is, and where you are in your business's development. Here's a framework for thinking through your choices.

If You're Primarily Chasing Homeowners

Houzz should be your first investment — create a complete profile, upload professional photos, and actively request reviews from satisfied customers. It's free to list and the audience is explicitly home-renovation-focused, which means every person who finds you there has already declared intent. A Houzz Pro subscription ($60–$100/month) adds lead-generation features that many shops find worth the cost once their profile has reviews.

Instagram is your second priority. Visual trades perform strongly on Instagram, and a well-curated feed of your work — particularly process photos and before/after sequences — can generate significant organic reach. We'll cover Instagram strategy in detail in Chapter 4.

Google Business Profile (formerly Google My Business) is free and essential. Every homeowner who searches "custom cabinets [your city]" will see it. Make sure it's complete, has your current hours and contact information, and has recent photos. Actively solicit Google reviews — they directly affect your ranking in local search results.

If You're Building Designer Relationships

Personal outreach beats any marketing channel when it comes to designers. Identify the five to ten kitchen and bath designers in your market who serve the homeowner demographic you want to reach. Visit their studios in person with a physical portfolio. Offer a shop tour. Attend NKBA events. This is relationship sales, and it happens in person — not through Instagram ads.

If You're Pursuing Contractor Work

General contractors find vendors through referrals from other contractors, through previous direct experience, and through presence on platforms like BuildZoom or contractor-focused networks. Being active in your local Home Builders Association (HBA) chapter is often the most direct path — it puts you in the same room as the buyers.

Channel Priority by Stage

If you're in early growth (under $500K annual revenue), your priority order should be: (1) complete and optimize your Google Business Profile, (2) create a Houzz profile with professional photos, (3) build a basic but high-quality website with a portfolio, (4) ask every satisfied customer for a Google review. This costs almost nothing and establishes the foundation everything else builds on.

If you're in the growth phase ($500K–$1.5M), add Instagram with a real content strategy, consider Houzz Pro, and begin the personal outreach to two to three key designer relationships. Paid advertising (PPC) may make sense at this stage, but only after the organic foundation is solid.

CHAPTER 4
YOUR DIGITAL PRESENCE

Your digital presence is usually the first impression a potential customer forms of your business. For most shops, that means a website, a Google Business Profile, a Houzz listing, and Instagram. Getting these right doesn't require a marketing agency or a large budget. It requires understanding what each platform is for and using it accordingly.

Your Website: The Foundation

Your website has one job: to convince someone who found you that you're worth calling. Everything else is secondary.

The single most important element on a cabinet shop website is the photo portfolio. Potential customers are trying to visualize whether you can produce what they want. A gallery of twenty to thirty high-quality project photos — properly lit, professionally photographed, showing the full range of your work — will do more for your conversion rate than any amount of copywriting. If you don't have professional photos of your work, hire a photographer. It's the best marketing investment most shops can make.

Portfolio photos should be filterable or organized by style (shaker, contemporary, traditional painted vs. stained) and by room (kitchen, bathroom, laundry, built-ins), so potential customers can quickly find examples that match what they're imagining. A 52-year-old homeowner planning a traditional kitchen should be able to find your traditional kitchen photos in under thirty seconds.

Beyond the portfolio, your website needs: a clear description of what you build and where you work, a simple contact form or consultation request mechanism, and enough information about your process to reduce the anxieties of a first-time buyer. What happens after they contact you? How long does the process take? What does a typical engagement look like? Answering these questions on your website eliminates objections before a consultation even happens.

One shop owner added a simple "How It Works" page to her website — four steps from initial inquiry to installation, with a realistic timeline at each stage and a note about what the customer would need to have ready. She tracked her consultation inquiries before and after. The volume didn't change, but the quality did: people who booked consultations after reading that page came in already understanding the process, asking better questions, and converting at a significantly higher rate. The page took her two hours to write.

Local SEO for Cabinet Shops

Search engine optimization for a cabinet shop is primarily a local exercise. You want to rank for searches like "custom cabinets [city]", "kitchen cabinet maker [city]", and "built-in shelving [city]" — not for generic national terms. Local SEO is driven by three things: your Google

Business Profile (keep it updated with new photos and respond to every review), consistent mentions of your city and surrounding towns throughout your website content, and the number and recency of your Google reviews.

Don't overthink technical SEO. A clean, fast-loading website with clear page titles, a few pages of genuine content about your services and location, and regular review acquisition will outperform a technically optimized but thin website every time.

3D Visualization and Online Tools

An increasing number of custom cabinet shops are incorporating 3D visualization tools into their client presentation process. Tools like 2020 Design, ProKitchen, or Cabinet Vision allow you to generate photorealistic renderings of a proposed design. Showing a customer their actual kitchen — with their countertop choice, their appliance layout, their door style — before they sign a contract dramatically reduces buyer anxiety and increases close rates.

Whether you put these renderings on your website or reserve them for the consultation stage is a strategic choice. Either way, if you're not offering some form of visualization and your competitors are, it's a gap worth closing.

Social Media: Instagram and Beyond

Instagram is the primary social media platform for visual trades, and cabinet shops that do it well generate genuine business from it. The shops that don't do it well post the same finished-project photo week after week and wonder why nobody engages.

The insight behind effective Instagram for a cabinet shop is this: people don't follow you to see your finished products. They can see finished products on your website. They follow you to see how you work — the material selection, the machine room, the detail of a dovetail joint being fit, the satisfaction of a perfect finish coming out of the spray booth. Process content outperforms product content on Instagram in this trade, consistently.

Posting the same project-after-project photo is not doing either of you a service. The relationship has to be interactive and engaging.

A practical Instagram content mix for a cabinet shop: 30% finished project reveals, 30% in-process work (shop floor, material prep, joinery details), 20% behind-the-scenes (your team, your tools, your shop), 20% customer-facing content (before/after sequences, client reaction moments, educational posts about materials or finishes). The mix keeps a feed interesting and builds a picture of who you are, not just what you make.

Instagram stories and Reels reach more people than static posts. A 30-second Reel of a reveal moment — empty kitchen to finished install — can generate more organic reach than a dozen still photos. You don't need video production experience. A smartphone, decent lighting, and genuine content are enough.

Houzz is different from Instagram. It functions more like a search engine than a social platform. Homeowners on Houzz are in planning mode, not browsing mode. A well-optimized Houzz profile with professional photos, clear service descriptions, your geographic coverage area, and a solid review count will generate inbound leads for years with minimal ongoing effort.

Paid Advertising: When It Makes Sense

Pay-per-click advertising through Google Ads can be effective for cabinet shops, but it's expensive and often not the right first investment. Clicks for search terms like "custom kitchen cabinets" cost $8–$25 each in most markets, and converting a click to a consultation typically requires 15–30 clicks. Do the math before you commit a budget.

PPC makes the most sense when: you have an established website with a strong portfolio and positive reviews (otherwise you're paying for traffic that won't convert), you're targeting a specific high-margin service (commercial millwork, a particular style you dominate), or you're trying to fill a capacity gap quickly. It is not a substitute for the organic foundation of Google reviews, Houzz presence, and website quality.

Facebook and Instagram paid advertising can work well for brand awareness and retargeting — showing your work to people who've already visited your website. The targeting capabilities (homeowners in specific zip codes, people who follow home renovation accounts) are useful. Start with a small budget ($300–$500/month) and measure carefully before scaling.

CliqStudios and similar larger cabinet companies use Google Ads heavily and have the budget to dominate broad search terms. Don't try to compete with them on generic terms. Compete on local intent: "[your city] custom cabinet maker" is a term they're probably not bidding on, and it's exactly what a local homeowner types.

Managing Your Online Reputation

Your Google reviews are more important than your website, your social media presence, and probably your advertising combined. For most potential customers, Google reviews are the first thing they check and the last thing standing between you and a consultation request.

The shops with 50+ reviews and a 4.8+ rating get called first. The shops with 11 reviews and a 4.2 get called when the 4.8 shop is booked. This is the reality of local service business reputation management.

Build review acquisition into your process as a standard

step, not an afterthought. After every successful project, ask for a Google review — in person at the end of the job, with a follow-up text that includes the direct link. Most satisfied customers will do it if you make it easy. A shop that asks consistently will build its review count steadily; a shop that hopes customers will review organically will stay stuck at twelve.

Respond to every review, positive and negative. Responding to positive reviews shows you're engaged. Responding to negative reviews — calmly, professionally, and briefly — shows potential customers that you take responsibility. A single negative review handled well rarely costs you business. A negative review that goes unanswered for six months costs you more than you realize.

CHAPTER 5
OFFLINE AND REFERRAL MARKETING

Digital marketing gets a lot of attention because it's measurable, scalable, and feels modern. But for most custom cabinet shops, the majority of their best business still comes from offline sources: a friend's recommendation, a contractor who's used you before, a designer who trusts your work. Understanding how to intentionally cultivate these channels — rather than just hoping they happen — is one of the highest-leverage things you can do for your business.

Referral Marketing: Your Most Important Channel

The single most powerful marketing channel for most custom cabinet shops is referrals. A homeowner referred by a friend who loved their kitchen is already 80% sold before they call you. They have trust that no advertisement can buy. They're more likely to proceed, less likely to negotiate aggressively on price, and more likely to refer others themselves.

The problem is that most shops treat referrals as something that happens to them rather than something they create. They do good work, hope customers tell their friends, and leave it at that. A referral system is different — it makes asking for referrals a routine part of the process, and it gives customers a reason to refer that goes beyond goodwill.

Asking Directly

The simplest and most effective referral tactic is the direct ask. At the end of a job — ideally at the final walk-through when the customer is standing in their new kitchen and feeling good about the result — say something like: "If you know anyone else planning a renovation, we'd love to work with them. Would you be comfortable mentioning us?" Most satisfied customers are happy to do this. Most never think to do it unless asked.

Follow up with a handwritten thank-you note after the project. Include a few business cards. It's a small gesture that stands out in an era of automated emails.

Referral Incentives

A structured referral program gives customers a reason to actively recommend you rather than just passively mention you. Practical options for cabinet shops include: a $200–$300 credit toward a future project for each referral that results in a signed contract, a hardware upgrade on their next project, or a cash thank-you payment for a referral that closes.

Keep it simple and clearly communicated. A referral program that requires customers to track codes or navigate a portal will see very low participation. One that says "refer someone who hires us and we'll give you $250 toward your next project" is clear, memorable, and motivating.

One shop owner formalized her referral program after noticing that three of her best customers had each sent her two or three referrals over the years — without any incentive, just because they were happy and generous. She called each of them, thanked them personally, and told them about the new program. Within six months, those same three customers had collectively sent her four new projects. The program didn't create referral behavior that wasn't there; it rewarded and amplified behavior that already existed.

Contractor and Builder Referral Networks

General contractors and builders who regularly need cabinet work are a different kind of referral source — they're ongoing, high-volume, and relationship-based. Building two or three strong GC relationships can provide a steady floor of work that helps you manage cash flow and capacity.

The approach is the same as with individual customers: do excellent work, communicate proactively, and make their life easier. But with contractors, the stakes are higher — a single bad experience with a deadline miss or a quality problem can end the relationship. Conversely, a contractor who trusts you becomes a genuine advocate, not just a repeat customer.

Be present where contractors gather: local Home Builders Association meetings, regional trade events, supplier showroom events. The cabinet shop owner who shows up consistently, introduces themselves, and follows up becomes a known name. The one who stays in the shop and hopes contractors find them waits a long time.

A note on GC margin discipline: one shop owner described taking on a large-volume contractor relationship that, on paper, looked attractive. The contractor sent steady work. What he didn't notice for the first year was that every job came with scope additions that weren't in the original price — extra trim work, last-minute hardware changes, installation timeline shifts that required overtime. By the time he ran the actual numbers, the relationship was costing him money. Know your floor, put everything in writing, and review the profitability of your GC work at least annually.

Kitchen and Bath Designer Partnerships

A single kitchen designer who specifies your cabinets on every project can generate six to fifteen jobs per year — all warm leads who've already been pre-sold on you by someone they trust. Designer partnerships are the highest-leverage referral relationship a custom shop can have.

Getting into a designer relationship starts with a personal introduction. Identify the designers in your market whose projects align with the quality and style of your work. Visit their studio, bring a physical portfolio, and offer a shop tour. Show them your process, your material samples, your finish room. The shop tour is often the turning point — a designer who walks through a well-organized, clean shop with skilled craftspeople comes away with confidence in you that no website can convey.

Maintain the relationship with communication and reliability. Designers talk to each other. One outstanding experience with a difficult job — delivered on time, perfectly finished, with proactive communication throughout — spreads through the design community faster than any advertisement.

Direct Mail

Direct mail is not dead. For a custom cabinet shop targeting homeowners in specific neighborhoods, a well-executed direct mail campaign can produce solid results at a lower cost per lead than digital advertising.

The most effective targeting approach is USPS Every Door Direct Mail (EDDM), which allows you to mail to every address in a selected carrier route. For a cabinet shop, target carrier routes in neighborhoods where the home values align with your pricing — a $40,000 custom kitchen is a hard sell in a neighborhood of $180,000 starter homes. Your local post office or a mail house can help you identify and select the right routes.

The mailer itself should lead with a single, compelling image of your best work — a finished kitchen that stops someone flipping through their mail. Include a clear call to action (a consultation offer, a special on a specific product), your website, and a phone number. A QR code linking to your portfolio works well for anyone who wants to see more before calling.

The most effective direct mail for cabinet shops tends to be before-and-after postcards: a split image showing an outdated kitchen and its replacement, with a caption that communicates the transformation. It's concrete, visual, and immediately relevant to anyone who walks into their own kitchen and thinks about what it could be.

Event Marketing and Showrooms

Home shows and local home improvement expos can be effective lead generators, particularly for shops that don't yet have a strong digital presence. The advantage is direct contact with homeowners who are actively in renovation-planning mode. The disadvantage is cost — booth fees, display materials, and staff time add up quickly.

If you exhibit at home shows, invest in a display that shows your work at its best. Don't bring brochures to a visual trade; bring samples of your best door styles, finish samples, and photos of completed projects. Give people something to touch. The tactile quality of well-made cabinetry is something no website can convey — use it.

An open house at your shop is often more cost-effective than a trade show. Invite past customers, local designers, and contractors for a Saturday morning. Show your facility, demonstrate your process, let people see how you work. A shop that looks like a place where serious work happens is a marketing asset in itself.

Print Marketing

Print marketing — brochures, mailers, and leave-behinds — plays a support role in a cabinet shop's marketing strategy. It's most effective as a closer: something a potential customer takes from an initial meeting that reinforces the impression you made in person.

A well-designed portfolio card or trifold brochure with high-quality photos of your work, your USP, and your contact information is a tool your sales team (even if that's just you) can leave at every consultation, give to every contractor who asks about your work, and drop at design studios. It costs more to produce than digital, but it has staying power — a homeowner may look at it again six months after a first conversation when they're finally ready to move forward.

Measuring the return on print is harder than measuring digital. Accept that limitation, keep the spend modest, and use it as part of a broader strategy rather than as your primary channel.

CHAPTER 6
SELLING CUSTOM WORK

Custom cabinet sales is not like selling a product off a shelf. The sales cycle is long — often three to nine months from first contact to signed contract. The purchase is high-stakes for the buyer. And the thing you're selling doesn't fully exist yet when the customer agrees to buy it, which means trust is doing most of the work that a physical product would otherwise do.

Understanding this changes how you approach the entire sales process. You're not trying to close a deal at the end of a consultation. You're trying to build enough trust, over enough time, that the decision to hire you feels obvious when the customer is finally ready.

The Cabinet Shop Sales Funnel

A sales funnel is simply the path a customer takes from first hearing about you to signing a contract. For a custom cabinet shop, that path has five stages: Awareness, Interest, Consideration, Decision, and Retention. The goal is to move customers through each stage intentionally, rather than hoping they find their way.

Awareness

The customer first becomes aware of your business — through a Google search, a referral, a Houzz listing, an Instagram post, a direct mail piece, or a contractor recommendation. At this stage, they're not evaluating you yet; they're just noting that you exist.

Your job at the awareness stage is to make a strong first impression. The quality of your photos the clarity of your Google Business Profile, the warmth of a referral from someone they trust — these are your tools. Don't waste the attention you earned with a weak website, outdated photos, or no online reviews.

Interest

The customer visits your website, scrolls your Instagram, or looks at your Houzz profile. They're beginning to evaluate whether you could be the right fit. This stage is often where cabinet shops lose people they could have won — not because their work isn't good, but because the digital presentation doesn't match the quality of what they build.

At the interest stage, offer something of value that doesn't require commitment. A free downloadable guide ("10 Questions to Ask Your Cabinet Maker Before You Sign Anything" is a real lead magnet that converts), a kitchen planning checklist, or an invitation to a no-pressure consultation all give the interested customer a reason to take a step toward you without the high stakes of a contract conversation.

Consideration

The customer is now actively comparing you against two or three other options. They're reading reviews, looking at your portfolio carefully, maybe asking their designer or contractor what they think. This is the stage where social proof does its heaviest lifting.

Make sure your Houzz profile and Google listing have recent, detailed reviews. Show case studies of projects similar to what this customer wants. If possible, offer a shop visit — a homeowner who has walked through your facility and met your team is 3–4 times more likely to hire you than one who's only seen your website. The in-person experience of a well-run shop is your single strongest sales tool.

Decision

The customer is ready to move forward. They're comparing your quote against one or two others, and they're making a final judgment about whether the price differential (if there is one) is justified by the difference in what they'll receive.

At this stage, clarity is everything. Your quote should be detailed enough to compare line-by-line with a competitor's. Your process should be clearly documented: what happens when, what they need to provide, what you'll provide, and what the payment schedule looks like. Ambiguity at the decision stage kills deals — not because the customer doesn't want to proceed, but because uncertainty feels riskier than the known alternative.

A clear, easy-to-use mechanism for signing — DocuSign or a simple online form — removes friction from the final step. Don't make a decided customer chase you to figure out how to give you money.

Retention

The job is done. The customer is standing in their new kitchen. This is not the end of the sales process — it's the beginning of the referral cycle. A follow-up survey, a personal thank-you note, and a direct ask for a Google review should be standard practice after every completed project. The customer who feels genuinely appreciated after the job is the customer who tells their neighbor about you.

Sales Best Practices

The first and most important rule of selling custom cabinet work is to listen before you pitch. When a customer contacts you, they have a problem (a kitchen that doesn't work, a bathroom with no storage, a renovation plan that needs execution) and a set of anxieties about getting that problem solved. Understanding both before you say anything about your capabilities is the foundation of a successful consultation.

One question changes every consultation: "Tell me what prompted you to finally decide to do this project." The answer tells you the real motivation — it may be a growing family, a house they're planning to sell, a renovation they've been putting off for a decade. Every answer changes the right approach. A customer selling their house in six months needs a quick-turn project with excellent finish quality. A customer who's been dreaming about their kitchen for twelve years needs the full design experience. The same pitch to both is the wrong pitch.

Address objections early rather than waiting for them to kill the deal. The four most common objections in custom cabinet sales are price ("this costs more than I expected"), timeline ("I need it done before Thanksgiving"), trust ("how do I know the finished product will match what I was shown"), and disruption ("I can't live without a kitchen for three months"). If you bring these up yourself and address them directly, you take their power away as late-stage deal-killers.

On price specifically: don't apologize for your pricing, and don't discount reflexively. Discounting signals to the customer that you were overcharging in the first place, or that your price is negotiable — neither of which you want to communicate. Instead, explain what the price buys: the material quality, the process, the finish, the guarantee. If a customer genuinely can't afford you, it's better to know that early and part on good terms than to discount yourself into a job that doesn't make financial sense.

A shop owner in the Pacific Northwest described a consultation with a homeowner who pushed hard on his price — said she'd gotten a quote from another shop that was $6,000 lower. Instead of matching it, he asked: "Can I show you the difference?" He walked her through his material specifications, his drawer box construction, his finish process, and his warranty. He didn't knock the competitor. He just made his own case with specifics. She hired him. When the other shop's cabinets went into a neighbor's kitchen a few months later with finish issues, she told that neighbor about her experience. Two referrals from a customer he almost discounted to close.

Measuring Sales Effectiveness

You can't improve what you don't measure. The good news is that you don't need to track twenty metrics. These five tell you almost everything you need to know about the health of your sales process:

Close rate. What percentage of consultations convert to signed contracts? A strong cabinet shop close rate is 35–50%. If yours is below 25%, something is breaking down in the consultation process — price, trust, process clarity, or all three.

Lead source. Where did each new customer first find you? Track this for every project. After six months you'll know which channels are generating your best customers, which lets you invest more in what works.

Average project value. Know your average revenue per project, and track whether it's growing or shrinking. If it's shrinking, you may be attracting lower-budget customers, or you may be discounting more than you realize.

Sales cycle length. How many days from first contact to signed contract? For homeowners, 30–90 days is typical. Significantly longer may indicate a follow-up process that's falling down; significantly shorter may indicate you're leaving qualification steps out and signing customers who later become problems.

Customer acquisition cost. Divide your total marketing spend (including your time) in a period by the number of new customers acquired. This tells you what you're actually paying to get a customer, which is essential context for any marketing budget decision.

For tracking, you don't need expensive software. A simple spreadsheet with a row per lead and columns for date, source, project type, quote amount, close/lost, and revenue covers the basics. If you want something more robust, tools like HubSpot (free tier), Jobber, or CoConstruct are designed for trade businesses and handle client communication, quoting, and project management in one place.

CHAPTER 7
SERVICE, RETENTION, AND REFERRALS

In the cabinetry business, customer service is not a soft concept. It's a revenue driver. A single satisfied customer who refers two neighbors generates more revenue than most marketing campaigns. A single dissatisfied customer who posts a detailed negative review can cost you more business than you'll ever know.

The stakes are high because the purchase is high-stakes. A homeowner who spends $35,000 on a new kitchen is not in a transactional mindset. They've invested a significant portion of their savings, they've endured weeks of disruption, and they are emotionally attached to the outcome. When something goes wrong — and in custom fabrication, something always eventually goes wrong — how you handle it determines whether you lose a customer or earn a loyal advocate.

Where Cabinet Shop Service Most Often Fails

The most common service failures in cabinetry are

predictable, and most of them are communication failures rather than quality failures.

The Communication Gap During Production

A homeowner signs a contract and then hears nothing for six weeks while their cabinets are being built. No updates, no photos, no confirmation that everything is on track. By week four, they're anxious. By week six, they're calling. By the time installation day arrives, they've already decided they probably won't refer you.

Fix this with a simple production update protocol: a brief email or text at the two-week mark confirming that production is on schedule (with a shop photo if possible), and a confirmation call one week before the installation date. That's it. Two touchpoints. The customer feels remembered, and their anxiety is managed before it becomes a complaint.

Installation Day Surprises

Nothing damages trust like arriving on installation day to find that a door color doesn't match the approved sample, a cabinet is 2 inches shorter than the customer expected, or the installer doesn't have the right hardware. These are quality and process failures, and they're preventable with rigorous pre-installation review.

Build a pre-installation checklist into your process: before the truck leaves the shop, every piece is checked against the job order, photos of each cabinet are taken, and any discrepancies are flagged and resolved before the installer is standing in someone's kitchen with the problem in hand. One delayed installation is better than one installation-day disaster.

Post-Job Silence

Most cabinet shops go quiet after the final invoice is paid. The customer has been in daily contact with you for months, and then nothing. This is a missed opportunity both for the relationship and for referrals.

A follow-up call or visit 30 days after installation — to ask how everything is working, whether there are any adjustments needed, and whether they're happy with the result — costs almost nothing and makes an impression that lasts. The customer who receives a 30-day follow-up call from their cabinet maker talks about it. It is genuinely unusual, and unusual service gets remembered.

Building a Service Culture

Excellent customer service isn't a policy. It's a culture — a set of expectations and behaviors that everyone in the shop shares, from the person answering the phone to the installer who's the last touchpoint a customer has with your business.

The installer is often the face of your company in the customer's home. An installer who is clean, professional, communicative, and respectful of the customer's space is a marketing asset. An installer who shows up late, leaves a mess, and gives one-word answers to questions is a liability regardless of how good the cabinets are. Train your installation team on customer interaction, not just technical installation.

Create clear service standards and communicate them: response time for inquiries (24 hours), escalation protocol for problems (call the customer before they call you), post-installation follow-up procedure, and how to handle a request that falls outside the original contract. When everyone knows the standard, consistency follows.

Customer Retention and Loyalty

Custom cabinet customers don't usually need another full kitchen in a year. But they might need a built-in bookcase in two years, a laundry room renovation in four, and a bathroom remodel in six. The homeowner who had a great experience with your kitchen is the perfect candidate for all three — if you stay in their awareness.

A simple annual touchpoint — a newsletter, a holiday card, an anniversary note on the one-year mark of their project — keeps you present without being intrusive. Most people don't find this annoying when it comes from a business they already trust; they find it reassuring. It says you're still here, you're still invested, and when they're ready for the next project, you'll be the first call.

A referral incentive program (covered in Chapter 5) is the other key retention tool. Frame it as a thank-you, not a transaction: "We loved working with you on your kitchen. If you ever refer a friend who hires us, we'd love to give you a $250 credit toward any future project as a thank-you." Clear, generous, and easy to share.

Handling Complaints

How you handle a complaint matters more than whether you get complaints. Every business that does enough volume will eventually have a customer who is unhappy. What separates the shops with 4.8-star averages from the shops with 3.9-star averages is not fewer problems — it's faster, more accountable responses to problems.

The principles: acknowledge the problem immediately (not defensively), take responsibility for your part in it (even if the customer's expectations were unreasonable, your process may have allowed those expectations to form), and propose a solution before being asked for one. Customers who feel heard and see you moving toward resolution almost never write negative reviews. Customers who feel dismissed — who have to argue for their complaint to be taken seriously — post reviews that cost you far more than the fix would have.

Navigating Difficult Situations

Every cabinet shop that operates long enough encounters situations that no process can fully prepare you for. The customer whose taste has shifted between contract and installation. The project delayed by a supplier that blows past the homeowner's holiday deadline. The door finish that looked perfect in the shop and looks wrong under the kitchen's pendant lighting. Knowing how to handle these moments is what separates a business with a strong reputation from one that's perpetually on the defensive.

When a Customer Changes Their Mind

It happens: a customer approves a door style and a stain color, production is well underway, and then she visits a friend's house and comes back wanting something different. This is one of the most delicate situations in custom cabinet sales because the customer feels like they have a right to change their mind — and to some extent, they do — while you have a legitimate financial exposure from work already done.

The best protection is a clear change order process built into your contract from the start. Any modification after production begins triggers a written change order with the cost of the change clearly stated and signed before any work is altered. This isn't adversarial — it's professional. Most customers, when they understand that their change request means real cost, either accept the change at that cost or decide they can live with their original choice.

When a change isn't possible because production is too far along, be honest and compassionate. "I understand this isn't what you're envisioning now, and I'm sorry. Here's what we can do at this stage" is a much better opening than a defensive recitation of the contract terms. Offer what genuinely is available — a different hardware choice, a different countertop, a different lighting option that pulls the look in the direction she's now seeing. You may not be able to give her everything she's changed her mind about, but you can show her that you're still working to get her to a result she loves.

When You Miss a Deadline

A delayed project is the complaint that generates the most emotional intensity, particularly when the homeowner has organized their life around a completion date — a holiday gathering, a home sale, a family event. The mistake most shops make is waiting too long to communicate the problem.

The rule is: the moment you know there's a risk to the timeline, you call the customer. Not when the delay is confirmed. When it's possible. A customer who gets a call three weeks before the expected completion saying "I want to let you know there's a supplier issue that may affect our timeline — I'm working on it and I'll have a clear answer for you by Thursday" is frustrated but feels respected. A customer who gets a call two days before the expected start of installation saying "we're going to be three weeks late" has been blindsided, and that feeling of being blindsided is often angrier than the delay itself.

When a delay happens, offer something concrete: an adjusted timeline with a buffer built in, a partial credit toward the final payment, or an upgraded hardware package at no charge. The gesture matters less than the intent it communicates — that you take the disruption seriously and you're taking ownership of it.

The Warranty Call a Year Later

A drawer front has shifted. A door hinge is squeaking. A finish has lifted in a corner where it meets the countertop. These are the calls that come months or a year after a job, and how you handle them shapes the long-term reputation of your business more than almost anything else.

A straightforward response — "Of course. Let me get

someone out to you this week" — is the right answer almost every time. The cost of sending an installer to adjust a few hinges is trivial. The cost of a customer who tells their network that your shop didn't stand behind its work is not.

Maintain a simple log of every warranty call by project: what the issue was, what caused it, and how it was resolved. Over time this log tells you things your quality control process can't — the door style whose finish tends to lift at certain temperature swings, the drawer slide that fails under heavy load, the installer who consistently leaves adjustments slightly off. Each warranty call is free diagnostic information about where your process or your materials need improvement.

The Emotional Reality of Custom Work

Custom cabinetry occupies an unusual place in the lives of the people who buy it. A new kitchen is rarely just a kitchen. It's the room where the family gathers. It's the renovation that a couple has been planning and arguing about and saving for over years. It's the project that a homeowner is doing to feel settled in a house they weren't sure they loved. The emotional investment in the outcome is genuinely high, and understanding that changes how you interact with customers at every stage.

It means that the homeowner who keeps emailing about small things — the placement of a pull, the reveal on a door — isn't being difficult. She's anxious about something she's spent a lot of money on and can't yet see. Reassure her. Send a shop photo. Invite her in for a progress look. The time it takes is small; the trust it builds is significant.

It means that the husband who seems disengaged during consultations while his wife does most of the talking often has opinions that haven't been surfaced. Ask him directly: "What's most important to you about how this turns out?" You may find he has strong feelings about the hardware, or the depth of the drawers, or something nobody has asked him about yet. Including him is good service and good selling.

It means that when a project is complete and a customer is standing in their new kitchen seeing it for the first time, that moment is worth acknowledging. Don't rush to collect the final payment and get to the next job. Stand there with them for a minute. Let it land. The pride you feel in the work and the joy they feel in the result is the whole point of the business — and a customer who experienced that moment with you becomes the most natural referral source you'll ever have.

CHAPTER 8
RUNNING THE SHOP

Everything in the previous chapters — the marketing, the sales, the customer service — is what fills your order book. This chapter is about what happens on the other side of that: the operations, finance, and people management that determine whether a full order book translates into a profitable, sustainable business or just a lot of busy, stressful work.

This chapter provides a practical overview, not an exhaustive treatment. Business planning, financial management, and human resources are topics that fill entire libraries. What follows is what matters most specifically for a custom cabinet shop — the things that general business books either skip entirely or address at a level of abstraction that doesn't help you run a three-bay shop with five employees.

Business Planning

A business plan for a cabinet shop doesn't need to be a 40-page document unless you're seeking outside financing. What it does need to be is an honest, written answer to the questions that most shop owners carry around in their heads but never write down: Where are we going? How are we going to get there? What are we working toward?

The mission and vision are where you start. What does your shop exist to do, and what does success look like in five years? Specific is better than vague — "build the most respected custom cabinet shop in the greater Columbus market" is a mission you can actually test decisions against. "Provide quality cabinetry solutions" is not.

The financial and operational goals follow from the mission. If your five-year goal is $1.5M in annual revenue, what does that mean for your current capacity? How many jobs do you need to run simultaneously? How many employees? What equipment? Working backwards from the target to the present is how a plan actually guides decisions rather than just sitting in a drawer.

See Appendix A6 for a business plan outline that you can adapt for your shop.

Financial Management: What Actually Matters for a Cabinet Shop

Job Costing

The single most important financial practice for a custom cabinet shop is job costing — tracking the actual materials and labor cost of each project against the estimate. Without job costing, you have no idea whether a given type of project (full kitchen, bathroom vanity, built-in shelving) is actually profitable, and no basis for improving your estimates.

The mechanics are simple: for each job, record what you estimated for materials and labor, and what you actually spent. Compare them. Do this for every job for six months, and patterns will emerge. You'll find the project type you consistently underestimate, the material that almost always runs over, the installation variable you keep forgetting to price in. Every one of those patterns is money you've been leaving on the table.

The goal of job costing is not to find out you were wrong — it's to improve your estimates until they're accurate enough to price confidently. A shop with accurate estimates prices competitively where it can and confidently where it should, rather than guessing and hoping.

Cash Flow Management

The cash flow challenge in cabinetry is structural: you buy materials before you build, you build for weeks before you install, and you often collect final payment after installation. That gap — between when money goes out and when money comes in — is what kills profitable shops that don't manage it carefully.

The standard solution is a draw schedule built into every contract: 30–40% at signing, 30–40% at start of production, and the balance at delivery or installation. This is normal practice in the industry and customers expect it. A shop that collects 100% at completion is financing its customers' renovations, and most shops don't have the cash reserves to do that sustainably.

Maintain a cash flow projection that shows you, at any point, what you expect to receive and spend over the next 90 days. It doesn't need to be precise — a reasonable estimate updated monthly is enough to avoid being surprised. The shops that run into cash crises rarely do so because they aren't profitable; they run into them because they didn't see the crunch coming far enough in advance to act.

Understanding Your Shop Rate

Your shop rate is the hourly cost of running your shop, used to estimate labor on any given project. It's calculated by taking your total fixed and variable overhead (rent, utilities, equipment depreciation, insurance, admin) plus your desired owner compensation, dividing by the number of billable hours your shop produces in a year, and adding your target margin.

Most cabinet shops that struggle financially have never actually calculated their shop rate. They estimate labor by feel — "that job's about 40 hours" — without knowing what 40 hours actually costs them to produce. Calculate your shop rate once, verify it annually, and use it as the floor for every estimate you write.

Here's a straightforward calculation. Take a shop with two full-time craftspeople and one part-time installer. Annual overhead: $36,000 (rent $18K, utilities $4K, insurance $6K, equipment and maintenance $5K, admin and software $3K). Owner's target salary: $72,000. Total cost to cover before profit: $108,000. The two full-time employees together produce roughly 3,200 billable shop hours per year (accounting for holidays, maintenance days, and non-billable time). Divide $108,000 by 3,200 hours: $33.75 per hour just to break even. Add a 25% margin for reinvestment and profit: $42.19 per hour. That's the shop rate. A job estimated at 40 shop hours needs to price the labor component at a minimum of $1,688 — before materials. Many shops in this situation are charging half that, and wondering why they can't get ahead.

For reference: a well-run custom cabinet shop should achieve a gross margin (revenue minus materials and direct labor) of 45–60%. Net profit after overhead should be 10–18%. If your numbers are consistently below these ranges, the problem is either pricing or costs — and job costing will tell you which.

Equipment Financing

A CNC router, an edge bander, or a downdraft finishing table can transform your production capacity — but these are capital investments, not operating expenses. Finance them accordingly: equipment loans or lines of credit with terms matched to the useful life of the equipment (5–7 years for most shop machinery). Don't buy capital equipment out of operating cash flow if it creates a cash squeeze on your current jobs.

SBA 7(a) loans are available for small manufacturers and can finance both equipment and working capital at favorable rates. Your bank or a local SBDC (Small Business Development Center) can walk you through eligibility. The application process is involved, but the rates and terms are often significantly better than commercial equipment financing.

Knowing When to Say No

One of the most valuable business skills a cabinet shop owner can develop is the ability to decline work — and to do it without guilt. A full schedule is not the same as a profitable schedule, and the jobs you don't take are sometimes as important to your business health as the ones you do.

There are four categories of work worth declining or approaching with serious caution. The first is the chronically low-margin job: work priced below your shop rate that you're tempted to take because the shop is slow. Filling capacity with unprofitable work delays the real solution (more leads, better pricing) while consuming the time and energy that would otherwise go toward finding it.

The second is the misaligned customer — someone whose expectations, communication style, or budget is fundamentally incompatible with how you work. A customer who argues over every line item before the contract is signed will not become easier to work with after it's signed. A customer who clearly wants a semi-custom big-box result at a custom price is not your customer, no matter how much they want to be. Recognizing this early and declining gracefully — "I want to make sure we're the right fit for what you're looking for, and I think you'd be better served by [X]" — protects both parties.

The third is the job with a timeline that your current capacity can't honestly meet. Taking work you can't deliver on time damages your reputation regardless of how good the finished product is. Better to be honest about your lead time and offer a future start date than to overpromise and end up with an angry customer and an overextended team.

The fourth is work outside your real capabilities. Every shop has a range of work it does excellently and work it does adequately. The job that requires a finish technique you haven't mastered, a wood species your finishing room struggles with, or a production volume beyond your realistic capacity is better referred to a colleague than accepted and delivered below your standard. The referral builds goodwill with the colleague and protects your reputation with the customer.

Human Resource Management

For most cabinet shops, the team is small — two to ten people — and the HR challenges are correspondingly human-scale. You're not managing a corporation; you're managing craftspeople. What matters most is finding the right people, keeping them, and creating a shop culture where good work is expected and recognized.

Hiring

The cabinet trade has a workforce challenge: skilled craftspeople are increasingly hard to find, and the pipeline from trade schools and vocational programs is thin. This means you can't afford to wait for the perfect candidate to walk in. Build relationships with local community college woodworking programs, vocational schools, and community maker spaces. Offer apprenticeships or paid internships. The cabinetmaker you hire at 19 and train over three years is often more loyal and more skilled, for your specific process, than the experienced hire from three shops over.

When hiring, evaluate attitude and trainability alongside skill. A mediocre craftsman who is reliable, communicative, and coachable will outperform a technically excellent one who is difficult, unpredictable, or unwilling to follow process. You can teach joinery; you cannot teach character.

Retention

Retention in a small cabinet shop is primarily about four things: fair pay, clear expectations, genuine recognition, and a sense of future.

Fair pay means knowing what comparable shops in your market pay and matching or beating it. You cannot afford to lose a skilled finisher to a competitor over $2 an hour. Pay competitively, and review wages annually rather than waiting for someone to give notice.

Clear expectations mean that every person in the shop knows exactly what excellent performance looks like in their role, and what the consequences of consistent underperformance are. Performance conversations are uncomfortable but far less painful than the alternative of carrying underperforming employees indefinitely because the conversation was never had.

Recognition in a small shop is mostly personal. Acknowledge excellent work in the moment. Bring the team together when a particularly good job ships. Share positive customer feedback — "The Harrington kitchen installed last week, the customer sent a message saying it was the most beautiful thing they'd ever had in their home" — and mean it. People who feel their work matters stay in jobs where their work is seen.

A sense of future means that employees can see a path forward with you. Cross-training on CNC operation, the opportunity to lead an installation team, involvement in material selection and shop decisions — these things cost you almost nothing and matter enormously to someone deciding whether to stay or leave.

Training and Development

The cabinet industry is changing faster than it has in decades. CNC manufacturing, new finish chemistries, software-driven design tools — a shop that isn't actively developing its team's skills is falling behind. Build training into your annual rhythm: budget for one or two employees to attend a trade event (AWFS Fair, IWF, regional KCMA events) per year. Invest in software training when you adopt new tools. Create a culture where learning is expected rather than incidental.

Cross-training across functions — shop, finishing, and installation — improves flexibility and reduces your vulnerability to any single person's absence. It also gives employees a broader view of the business, which tends to increase their investment in the outcome.

CHAPTER 9
KEEPING THE CRAFT ALIVE

All of the advice in this book — the customer profiling, the USP development, the sales funnels, the job costing, the retention strategies — exists for one reason: to give you a business strong enough to protect the work you love doing.

The cabinetmaker who builds a thriving business doesn't have to take every job that calls. They can say no to the customer who haggles over every line item, no to the contractor who wants their timeline and their pricing without any flexibility, no to the project that would crowd out something more interesting. Financial and operational strength doesn't just mean profit — it means the freedom to do the work you're proud of, with the customers who value it, at the price it deserves.

That's the goal. Not a business that survives, but a business that gives you a real choice in what you build and who you build it for.

Start with the chapter or two most relevant to where your business is right now. Don't try to implement everything at once — a business that improves by 10% in five areas over a year has transformed itself. Pick the highest-leverage problem, fix it completely, and move to the next one.

The appendix contains templates and surveys you can put to work immediately. The customer satisfaction survey, the pre-project questionnaire, and the financial plan outline are all ready to adapt to your shop. Use them.

There's a line I've heard from experienced cabinetmakers more times than I can count: the work teaches you if you let it. The same is true of the business. Pay attention to what your numbers are telling you, to what your customers are telling you, to what your employees are telling you. The shop that stays teachable — that treats every slow month and every service failure and every departed employee as information rather than just bad luck — is the shop that gets better over time.

The cabinetmakers I've seen build genuinely strong businesses share a few traits that have nothing to do with marketing or finance. They're honest with themselves about where their business is. They're willing to have uncomfortable conversations — about pricing, about underperforming employees, about customers who aren't the right fit — rather than letting problems drift. They take the business seriously without losing sight of why they got into the trade in the first place.

And they protect their time in the shop. Not as an escape from the business, but as the source of everything the business is built on. The owner who never has a chisel in their hand anymore, who spends every day on estimating and emails and scheduling, often loses something important — the direct feel for what the work costs, what it requires, what makes it worth doing. The businesses I've admired most are run by people who still know what a tight-fitting joint feels like, who still stop to look at a finished piece before it goes out the door. That connection to the work keeps the business honest.

Build a business worth staying in. The craft deserves it, and so do you.

Best regards,
Jason

APPENDIX

The following tools are designed to be used, not just read. Copy them, adapt them to your shop's voice, and build them into your standard process

A1. Pre-Project Customer Survey

Use this survey at or before the initial consultation to understand what a potential customer is looking for and how to tailor your presentation to their priorities. Deliver it via email ahead of a scheduled consultation, or use it as a conversation guide.

1. What is your primary reason for considering custom cabinetry? (Storage, aesthetics, renovation, home value, other)

2. Which room or rooms are you planning to address? (Kitchen, bathroom, laundry, bedroom, home office, other)

3. What style resonates most with your vision? (Traditional/shaker, contemporary, transitional, rustic, painted, other)

4. Which materials are you drawn to? (Solid wood species, painted MDF, laminate, glass accents, other)

5. How important is price in your decision relative to quality and timeline? (Price-first, balanced, quality-first)

6. Which features are most important to you? Select all that apply: Soft-close hardware, pull-out shelves, custom sizing, interior lighting, specialty storage (spice drawers, trash pull-outs, etc.)

7. Do you have specific requirements — ceiling height considerations, appliance clearances, unusual dimensions, accessibility needs?

8. What is your target timeline for project completion?

9. Have you worked with a custom cabinet shop before? If yes, what went well and what didn't?

10. What is the best way to reach you, and what is your preferred communication style (email, phone, text)?

A2. Post-Project Satisfaction Survey

Send this survey within two weeks of project completion. Keep it short — five to eight questions max — to maximize response rates. Consider offering a small incentive (hardware credit, entry into a drawing) for completion.

11. On a scale of 1–10, how satisfied are you with the overall quality of the finished cabinetry?

12. Did the project stay on or close to the quoted timeline? If not, were delays communicated proactively?

13. How would you rate the communication you received during the build and installation process? (1 = never heard from them, 10 = always kept informed)

14. Was the installation team professional and respectful of your home?

15. Were there any issues during the project? If yes, how well were they resolved?

16. How likely are you to recommend us to a friend or family member? (1–10)

17. Is there anything we could have done better? Please be direct — we use this feedback to improve.

18. Would you be willing to share a photo of the finished space that we could use in our portfolio? (Y/N — permission required)

A3. Follow-Up Phone Script

Use this as a guide for the 30-day post-installation follow-up call. The goal is not to sell anything — it's to confirm the customer is happy, catch any small issues before they fester and plant the seed for a referral conversation.

"Hi [Name], this is [Your Name] from [Shop Name]. I wanted to call personally to check in — it's been about a month since we finished your [kitchen/bathroom/etc.] and I wanted to make sure everything is working the way it should."

[Let them respond. Listen for any issues and take notes.]

If there are issues: "Thank you for telling me — that's exactly why I called. Let me get [installer/shop manager] to reach out to you this week and get that sorted out."

If all is well: "I'm really glad to hear it. That project turned out beautifully. We really enjoyed working on it."

"One more thing — if you ever have a friend or neighbor who's thinking about a renovation project, we'd love the introduction. And if you'd be willing to leave us a quick Google review, it genuinely helps other homeowners find us and it means a lot to our small team. I can text you a direct link right now if that's easier."

"Thanks again, [Name]. We hope you're enjoying the space."

A4. Sales Funnel — Cabinet Shop Overview

The five stages of the cabinet shop sales funnel, with the primary tool and goal at each stage:

AWARENESS → Google / Houzz / Referral / Instagram / Direct Mail — Goal: Strong first impression

INTEREST → Website portfolio / Consultation offer / Lead magnet — Goal: Low-commitment next step

CONSIDERATION → Reviews / Shop visit / Case studies / Designer references — Goal: Build trust and reduce risk

DECISION → Detailed quote / 3D rendering / Clear contract / Draw schedule — Goal: Remove friction and ambiguity

RETENTION → Follow-up call / Thank-you note / Referral ask / Google review request — Goal: Turn customer into advocate

A5. Customer Service Standards Template

Adapt this template to your shop. Post it where your team can see it. Review it annually.

- Response time: All customer inquiries answered within 24 business hours
- Production updates: Customer contacted at the 2-week mark and 1 week before installation
- Issue escalation: Customer is called before they call us — any known problem is communicated proactively

- Installation standard: Installer arrives within 30 minutes of the communicated window; space is left as clean as it was found
- Post-installation follow-up: Follow-up call within 30 days of project completion
- Review request: Google review link sent after the follow-up call confirms satisfaction
- Complaint handling: Any complaint acknowledged within 4 business hours; resolution proposed within 48 hours

A6. Business Plan Outline

A complete business plan for a custom cabinet shop covers seven areas. Each can be expanded or condensed depending on your purpose (internal roadmap vs. outside financing application).

1. Executive Summary — Mission, vision, ownership structure, two-sentence description of what makes your shop different
2. Company Description — Services offered, geographic market, target customers (homeowner / designer / contractor), competitive position
3. Products and Services — Cabinet types, material options, custom capabilities, design services, installation, your USP
4. Marketing and Sales — Target customer profiles, primary marketing channels, sales process, referral strategy, pricing approach
5. Operations and Management — Shop layout, production capacity, equipment, key roles and responsibilities, process for quoting and project management
6. Financial Plan — Revenue projections, COGS and

gross margin targets, operating expenses, cash flow projection, break-even analysis, financing needs

7. Supporting Documents — Portfolio samples, key team resumes, any existing contracts or supplier agreements, market research data

A7. Financial Reference — Cabinet Shop Benchmarks

The following benchmarks apply to custom cabinet shops in the $300K–$1.5M annual revenue range. Use them to evaluate your own performance and identify where improvement would have the most impact.

Gross margin target: 45–60% (revenue minus materials and direct labor). Below 40% typically indicates underpricing, overbidding on materials, or labor inefficiency.

Net profit target: 10–18% after all overhead. Below 8% is a warning sign that overhead is too high relative to revenue.

Materials as % of revenue: 25–35% is typical for custom work. Significantly higher suggests pricing is too low or material waste is uncontrolled.

Labor as % of revenue: 25–35%, including benefits and payroll taxes. Labor costs that creep above 38% typically indicate quoting underestimates or scope creep.

Draw schedule (standard): 35% at signing / 35% at start of production / 30% at delivery or installation

Cash reserve target: 60–90 days of operating expenses held in liquid reserves to manage seasonal cash flow variation

Sample annual P&L — shop doing $1,000,000 in revenue:

- Revenue: $1,000,000
  - Materials: $280,000 (28%)

- Direct labor (shop + installation): $290,000 (29%)
- Gross profit: $430,000 (43%)
- Overhead (rent, utilities, insurance, equipment, admin): $185,000 (18.5%)
- Owner compensation package: $125,000 draw + $42,000 in business-paid benefits (see below)
- Net profit before tax: $120,000 (12%)

Understanding What the Owner Actually Earns

The $125,000 owner draw in the example above is the line item on the P&L. But for most cabinet shop owners structured as an S-Corp or LLC, it significantly understates what the business is actually providing. A realistic accounting of the owner's total compensation package looks something like this:

- Owner draw / salary: $125,000
- Health, dental, and vision insurance (owner + family): $18,000–$24,000/year
- Vehicle (payment, insurance, fuel, maintenance — business use): $10,000–$14,000/year
- Cell phone: $1,500–$2,400/year
- Retirement contributions (SEP-IRA or Solo 401k): $10,000–$25,000/year
- Professional development, trade events, subscriptions: $3,000–$5,000/year

Add those up and the total compensation value is realistically $167,000 to $195,000 per year — not $125,000. A W-2 employee receiving $125,000 in salary pays for all of those items out of pocket, after tax. The shop owner receives them as pre-tax business expenses. That distinction is real money.

This matters for two reasons. First, it means shop

owners often underestimate what they're actually earning, which distorts their sense of whether the business is performing. Second — and this is where many shop owners make a costly mistake — it completely changes the math when you're thinking about hiring someone to take work off your plate.

The Case for a Operations Manager

At some point in a growing cabinet shop, the owner becomes the bottleneck. They're quoting jobs, managing production, handling customer calls, ordering materials, training new hires, solving installation problems, and running the finishing schedule — all simultaneously. The business can only grow as fast as one person can context-switch, which isn't very fast and isn't very sustainable.

The solution is a qualified operations manager, production lead, or senior craftsman who can own a significant portion of the day-to-day. Someone who can train and organize labor, run the production floor without constant supervision, identify process problems before they become customer problems, and free the owner to focus on estimating, customer relationships, and business development — the activities that actually drive revenue.

The hesitation is always the cost. A manager or lead craftsman capable of running a $1M cabinet shop's production operation commands $100,000 to $120,000 in salary. That's a real number on the P&L, and for an owner accustomed to doing that work themselves, it can feel unjustifiable.

Here's the reframe: that manager receives $100,000–$120,000 in cash salary and nothing else. No vehicle. No family health insurance. No retirement contributions paid by the business. No phone. Their $110,000 salary is their total compensation. The owner's $125,000 draw, once you include the business-paid benefits itemized above, is worth

$167,000–$195,000 in equivalent W-2 terms. The owner is not cheaper than the manager. They are roughly equivalent in cost — and the owner's time is better spent on the activities that grow the business than on the ones the manager can handle.

Put another way: if hiring a $110,000 operations manager frees the owner to pursue two additional $150,000 kitchen projects per year that wouldn't have happened otherwise, the hire paid for itself and then some. The math works. The hesitation is psychological, not financial.

The right hire at this stage is someone with genuine production management experience — ideally from a cabinet shop or a similar custom manufacturing environment. They need to understand material flow, job scheduling, labor management, and quality control. They need to be the kind of person who finds disorder uncomfortable and building systems satisfying. They are not common, and when you find one, pay them what they're worth. The cost of losing a strong operations manager and rebuilding that capability is far higher than the cost of retaining them.

Run your own P&L with real numbers and compare each line to these benchmarks. Be honest about the full value of your owner compensation package — not just the draw. And when you find yourself doing work that a well-hired manager could do better, treat that as the financial opportunity it actually is.

Afterword

Dear Reader,

Thank you for reading this far. You invested real time in this book, which means you're serious about building something — and I respect that.

I want to leave you with one thought. Every tool in this book — the marketing strategies, the financial frameworks, the service standards — is in service of a single outcome: a business that is strong enough to let you do excellent work, on your terms, for as long as you want to do it.

That outcome is achievable. It doesn't require a large marketing budget, a business degree, or a personality transplant. It requires clear thinking about what your business is, who it serves, and what it costs to run. It requires the willingness to look at the numbers honestly and act on what they tell you. And it requires the patience to build systematically rather than lurching from one busy season to the next slow one.

Many of the best cabinet shops I've encountered are run by people who would never describe themselves as businesspeople. They'd say they're cabinetmakers. But the busi-

AFTERWORD

nesses they've built — disciplined, clear-eyed, genuinely profitable — reflect a kind of business intelligence that they developed by paying attention over years. That intelligence is available to anyone willing to develop it.

The trade has given a lot to a lot of people. Beautiful kitchens where families have gathered. Custom pieces that outlast the people who commissioned them. Work that requires real skill and produces something real. That's worth protecting, and protecting it requires more than just being good at it.

Build the business. Take care of the craft. They are not in opposition — they're partners.

All the best,
    Jason

annunci in pareggio o redditizi sono uno strumento incredibilmente prezioso. Naturalmente, la pubblicità online non è un segreto e non è facile. Molti operatori pubblicitari operano in perdita per indirizzare il traffico e le vendite verso i loro prodotti nella speranza che il marketing a pagamento alla fine crei uno slancio organico.

Indipendentemente dalla redditività oggettiva della spesa pubblicitaria, una persona con la capacità di migliorare l'efficacia degli annunci di un'azienda, indipendentemente da quale sia tale efficacia, vale un sacco di soldi per quell'organizzazione. Una persona che eccelle nella pubblicità a pagamento può indirizzare enormi quantità di traffico mirato verso siti Web di propria scelta e molti singoli imprenditori lo utilizzano nelle proprie attività.

Quindi, cosa comporta la pubblicità a pagamento? Generalmente, la pubblicità prevede un imbuto. Ogni funnel pubblicitario ha diverse fasi, che introducono le persone al marchio e all'azienda al livello più alto e le trasformano in clienti paganti al livello più basso. I funnel non hanno sempre bisogno di essere incanalati verso un punto di acquisto, ma solo verso i KPI identificati nelle sezioni del marchio e della strategia social. Si consideri, ad esempio, il seguente funnel di un'azienda teorica:

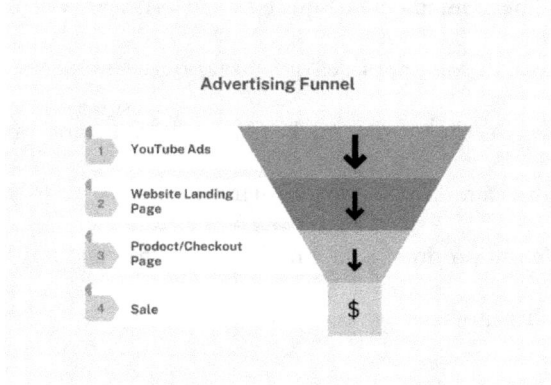

www.ingramcontent.com/pod-product-compliance
Lightning Source LLC
LaVergne TN
LVHW012036060526
838201LV00061B/4629